The Annihilation
of
Black America:

A Collection of Academic Writings

Nigisti HiSmith

ISBN: 978-0-578-34771-4

DEDICATION

I dedicate this book to our ancestors who endured, to
those who've lost their lives, and to
Black America.

CONTENTS

PREFACE

Maya Angelou wrote of the lost treasures of Africa. I'm naming the lost treasure: Black America. We are found deeply planted within the systems that created the "American Dream". Driven by greed for power and wealth. Our story does not begin on the wings of enslavement. It begins at the root of our mysterious African identity. Then labelled African American. To the trauma our ancestors endured, I reclaim the hope of rediscovering her lands and uncovering her dreams.

For how will we know if we are not educated? The past four US Presidents have openly declared, education is a civil right. However, legislatively it is far from the truth. Pearls of Grace, Inc. is a 501c4 civic and social awareness organization who advocates for women and children against the culprit, poverty. Making education a Civil Right is the assignment. Each American child should have the right to attend an educational institution that is safely built towards enhancing a child's knowledge, and wellbeing; not imprisoning them.

This book has been written to bring forth solutions to end the genocide of African Americans. Structurally vulnerable black communities have been laid to waste. Meanwhile, society is grooming our children to enter a profiting criminal system. American systems have not just assaulted Black America but have almost disintegrated it to its annihilation.

Chapter 1:

AFRICAN AMERICAN FEMALE
REPRODUCTION & INFANT MORTALITY

African American females have the highest rates of stress and infant mortality in the world. Components of negative life events, daily hassles, psychological distress and perceived stressors all make up the measures of stress experienced throughout pregnancy. Much of the black infant mortality is due to preterm birth, stress being a major contributor to preterm birth rates in African American women. Women who encountered higher levels of stress were almost two times more likely to experience a preterm delivery. Stress and racism are likely to being the culprit to preterm babies being born. Meanwhile, black women with college degrees encounter more racism than those without.

Sudden Infant Death Syndrome (SIDS) are found twice as high among African Americans. Most incidents happening between infant ages of 2-4 months due to families not following the recommended sleep positions. In 2001, Gessner, Ives and Perham-Hester found that,

"98% of infant deaths attributed to prone sleeping, sleeping with another person, or not in an infant crib. They further found that sleeping with another person in the prone position increased the risk for SIDS". There is a need for cultural care to be a major factor considered when health professionals are interacting with African American women. The unequal treatment of people of color broadens in healthcare when they are not provided with the "most sophisticated treatments" available compared to their Caucasian counterparts. Studies have found that more new African American mothers are apt to receiving instructions for proper handling of their baby when the nurse is respectful, nurturing, and demonstrates concern for the family. Due to the legacy of cultural mistrust between African Americans and Caucasians, additional time and care may need to be spent for the new mother and family to adhere to proper care for their baby. This builds bridges of trust and better care for African American women and their babies.

Yet, the negative impact of racism on sexual and reproductive health is an "underlying determinant" of social issues pertaining to disparities linked to poverty (I.e.: Education, employment, health) also includes African Americans are "2.8-3.7 times more likely to die from pregnancy-related complications compared with women of all other races/ethnicities". African American women receive lower quality healthcare due to Institutional racism. This has a lot to do with African Americans receiving limited care and education about issues regarding reproductive health. Familial and social stressors, internal racism, cultural mistrust, pregnancy-related morbidity and mortality are all factors to consider when it comes to obtaining and maintaining quality health during pregnancy for African American women.

Chapter 2:

BLACK TRAUMA, BLACK PARENTING & BLACK LEARNING

Many African American women are single mothers. Psychologists suggest that the child does not need to be worried with details about an absent parent that is not solvable until the child either inquires or has gone through the developmental stages. Doug Downey, PhD, a professor of sociology at Ohio State University, encourages single parents of the importance to obtain positive role models of the opposite sex to help communicate with the child during those often-uncomfortable topics pertaining to development. Yet, this is not to be mistaken for the distinction of a child's developmental outcome when a child grows up with a mother and father in the home.

There are three primary methods of how children learn. A child most often learns through either listening (auditory), looking (visual), or doing (kinesthetic). Most children learn from two of the three methods by giving examples of child behaviors from scenarios involving multiple backgrounds and environments. It is important to focus on strategies on how to increase the child's strengths.

For children living impoverished, there have been recent discovery showing that the project-based learning is the best option. Although each method of learning is special, auditory learners usually need quiet for concentration. They learn best by reciting information, repeating information or explaining information. Visual learners require order and quietness, showing the child shapes, colors and pictures. Kinesthetic learners typically learn with their bodies by moving around, touching and feeling items as they process information.

Parents can increase and sustain their children's motivation to learn in three primary areas. The first, is through a healthy desire to please, the second is through having a healthy attitude of perfectionism (doing one's best) and the third is through healthy competitiveness (with themselves). If parents still have a difficult time, remember that most children are eager to learn. However, since no two children learn exactly alike, ensure you have different ways to dispel the information composed.

Yet, there is a greater concern. Poverty and the outcome of prolonged impoverishment can be life altering. Poverty causes toxic stress not only to adults but also to children. The explanation of complex trauma in children stems also from non-effective parenting. These two elements combined affects children's behavior in several ways, such as willful disobedience, defiance, and inattention. The term Executive Function (EF) includes three functions in the development of a small child up to age six. These areas impacting functioning are Inhibitory Control, Cognitive Flexibility and Working Memory. The brain's memory storehouse is the Hippocampus. The emotional storehouse is the Amygdala. Chronic and recurrent stressful experiences from early childhood development is becoming more aware and is known as Toxic Stress. It has been proven Toxic Stress can have an adverse impact in brain architecture through hypertrophy and overactivity in the Amygdala, which can lead to a loss of neurons and neural connections in the brain.

Less brain development takes a toll on children living in impoverished, and high-stress environments with hostile parenting, low emotional support from guardians, and repeated exposure to stressful life events (Jack Shonkoff). The behavioral impacts of toxic levels of stress and is correlated to Altered Brain Architecture of children living in Early Adverse Experiences. The delay in development affects the linguistic, cognitive and social-emotional skills of children.

Often, adults are unaware with how to respond to a child who is living in Toxic Stress, and their inaccurate responses could impact the child far worse as it pertains to the educational process. This article proves that there is more of a need to increase Social and Emotional Learning (SEL) for adults and professionals who work with children, especially in marginalized communities.

Yet, there is a graver danger to our children. Prison is the gift of the present that is wrapped for the future of too many children of color. This is the national genocide of the African American. Prison negatively impacts the classroom, and it carries the potential to derail a child's future if their parent is the one who is incarcerated. As children with absentee parents look inward at other familial dynamics, too many children don't understand why their parent cannot be involved with them. The prison system in American undergone insurmountable growth starting in the early 1980s with roughly 350,000 prisoners to twenty years later over 2.1 million prisoners in 2000; majority being African Americans. Now, that there has been at least one generation of children who has been affected, new research of the effects of children with incarcerated is surfacing.

"In 1990, 1 in 4 black children born saw their father (predominate member) head off to prison before they turned 14." (Wildeman) Mental health issues, behavioral issues, and aggression are just a few results of children who face life with incarcerated parents. Studies say children are three times more likely to experience homelessness. Oppositional Defiant Disorder (ODD) has been diagnosed by professionals as the root cause being abandonment which transcribes into, I don't trust any other adult.

Researchers are concluding, "having a parent in prison makes it difficult – and sometimes impossible – to survive childhood's emotional roller coaster intact". And yet, when the child attends school, there is still no relief in sight. The National Center for Mental Health Promotion and Youth Violence Prevention, 2012 ran data from an Adverse Childhood Experience (ACE) study suggesting one in three children are most likely affected by early cases of childhood trauma. The constant stress of "chronic poverty" is also traumatic for children, as their guardians endure the continual stress of survival through adversity. (Leiberman & Osofsky, 2009) Children in these situations most often experience physical, mental and emotional neglect and abuse as guardians work out their frustrations of life.

By children attending school, it can be one place where the negative impact of living in a toxic environment can be turned around. Yet, among the insurmountable stress teachers carry with keeping up with the education standards, they are still in a position that can help reverse Toxic Stress their students may experience every day. However, most teachers nor administrators in American schools are not trauma certified to deal with the amount of trauma the next generation is coping with, resulting in more referrals to the Juvenile Justice system.

Yet, by being trauma certified, teachers can help

students form a safe outlet by forming a positive relationship with the children who are prone to display troubled behavior. Knowing and separating who the child is versus the behavior is paramount in redirecting the child's attention when acting out in a fit of rage. Teachers can also regulate emotional coping skills and behaviors by trying to understand what's behind the trauma through sensory-based activities. Thus, leading to resiliency and rehabilitation.

Adverse Childhood Experiences (A.C.E.'s) are negative experiences children encounter on the road of development. Incidents and accidents include various degrees of stress, acts of abuse and neglect for all humans. Research has indicated that individuals who experienced at least four Adverse Childhood Experiences tend to have a shorter life span of up to 20 years. The word trauma, derived from the 1960s Latin medical term meaning "physical wound… or a wound, a hurt; a defeat". Bing defines the word trauma as, "a deeply distressing or disturbing experience". According to Levine and Kline in their 2007 book titled, Trauma through a Child's Eyes, "Trauma happens when any experience stuns us… leaving us altered and disconnected from our bodies." Trauma happens at different levels for all people, what may be a traumatic event for one person may not necessarily be for the next person.

Trauma can occur in four categories: Physical, Psychologically, Physiologically and Emotionally. However, professionals agree that certain acts and events leave unprotected children to respond in a "fight, flight or freeze" response, which pertains to muscle memory in the body as a response to fear filled events. Over time, the Amygdala in the brain holds the memory attached to the feelings of fear and produces a delayed response, spurring on behaviors. Levine and Kline also write, "trauma is not in the event itself; rather, trauma resides in the nervous system."

Children most likely affected by trauma can vary across culture, class, and race. However, due to high criminal justice rates, lower educational opportunities, extended work hours, and poorer healthcare options in the African American community, single parent households take on additional pressure to raise children while living impoverished. Most are likely themselves to become subjected to trauma. Due to high incarceration rates, parents are unable to be with their children for extended amounts of time, which studies have now proven to produce toxic stress.

Incidents such as accidents and natural disasters usually happen once, and over time can create intense muscle memory of the event or anything that resembles the event. Children living in foster care due to abuse & neglect, and death. Children are more likely to be sexually abused when parents are away from their children for extended amounts of time. Unfortunately, parents or guardians who struggle with untreated mental illness, deal with substance abuse and encounter domestic violence in the home. With the divorce rates being over 50 percent, multiple households with children suffer in compounded ways.

Chapter 3:

THE HIDDEN REALITIES OF EDUCATION WHILE LIVING IN THE IMPOVERSHMENT DISPARITY

"African Americans rank behind all major racial/ethnic groups in annual household earnings (DeNavas-Walt, Proctor, & Lee, 2005)". Living in a perpetual state of survival often leads to 'toxic stress' and, "are three times likely to be poor" (U.S. Bureau of the Census, 1998). This review will inform readers on the realities of poverty in family life, and the mental/behavioral effects of poverty on children. The review also does its best to determine how poverty negatively impacts the lives of children and their future, based upon results from the Department of Juvenile Justice. More than likely, children raised impoverished are more likely to be referred into the juvenile justice system versus children raised in middle class.

Poverty, defined as being poor, along with living in a state of deprivation from goods and services that are essential to the maintenance of an adequate standard of living. The U.S. government spends just 10% of the national budget on kids – a fraction of what other developed countries spend. Children raised impoverished experience huger, unstable and sometimes harmful environments, emotional, physical and behavioral health issues. (Crosson-Tower, Cynthia pg.66) They face many challenges lacking necessary resources, proper support systems, and parental guidance than those of middle-class families. The US Census Bureau conducted an American Community Survey from 2010-2015 for Floridians and the research showed that, "Nearly 70% of families impoverished with children headed by a single-parent". African American families are most often living in impoverished communities, which leads to mothers spending less time with their children, resulting in their children having greater unsupervised time. The least educated racial/ethnic group are African Americans, and as single parents lack adequate resources to expose their children to better opportunities. Many live with and are being raised by grandparents, which means there is less emotional support with greater financial need. Many families living impoverished experience unstable home environments, which affect nutrition and daily needs. Impoverished communities alter its citizens differently as higher crime rates resurface, and communal housing issues perpetuate unhealthy relational attachments. Nevertheless, children observing these behaviors are most affected. Children living in impoverished neighborhoods typically lack space and resources for a community center or park for younger children, while middle to older aged children experience exposure pre-maturely to high rates of physical abuse, drugs and mental abuse.

However, children in middle-class households have a higher socio-economic status, which allots children the safety of daily needs met. They are likely to be raised by both parents, which provide children with better structure and emotional support; often resulting in less unsupervised time and better decision-making. It's proven that when a child's parent demonstrates love, support, and encouragement; children are better equipped to thrive under pressure and are less likely to act out. Due to middle-class families having more resources, children are just as likely to experience stress, however, in a different capacity.

Poverty is mental and social. For 13.5 percent of blacks, 10.9 percent of Hispanics, 5.8 percent of Asians and 4.3 percent of whites live in deep poverty here in the United States. There is new research is showing how children whose fathers who are incarcerated suffer from twice as many mental health issues than a child whose father is not. The NAACP reported, "In 2014 African Americans constituted 2.3 million, or 34% of the total 6.8 million correctional population". This is another component that adds to the realities of toxic stress because without additional support from a second parent, income levels and overall support in the home goes lacking. In cases of extreme poverty, coping is a higher activity by parents and other adults who are given charge to supervise children. Coping mechanisms such as drug and alcohol dependence leads to the highest cases of neglect; all issues which compound the mental health issues of children. Neglect leaves many children in a state of hopelessness, with a sense of feeling unloved within the family unit. In fact, only alcohol and drug abuse cite more detrimental results than poverty as a factor relating to child abuse (Jaudes & Voohis, 1995). The familial role of absent father, working mother repeats itself generationally and as additional stressors increase, so does substantiated cases of physical abuse reaching 6.6 percent and an increase in neglect reaching 12.6 percent.

Due to the disruptions and uncertainties of daily life that affect an impoverished family, it also affects the development of the brain and decreases the ability to achieve goals. Children in poorer communities are at a higher risk for physical health problems, for example: low birth rate, inadequate food supply, and risky behavior such as smoking or engaging in early sexual activity. Absent fathers and unemployed fathers are all associated with increased maltreatment. Poverty ultimately has a larger impact on neglect than on physical abuse. If single mothers work, child maltreatment is considerably more likely due to their high-stress levels, and they tend to be more neglectful/abusive.

Not all children who live impoverished will face the criminal justice system, but often live with risk factors that typically contribute to the outcome. In February 2018, a non-profit named Mother Jones published an article with statistics by People's Policy Project which reported, "In 2014, 57% of incarcerated men and 72% of incarcerated women had incomes below $22,500 before they were locked away". The Florida Department of Juvenile Justice does not directly report many statistics that relate to Florida children who are raised impoverished. However, many impoverished children are more than likely to be subjected to negative interactions in the DJJ (Department of Juvenile Justice). Yet, to help remove the stigma and dispel the "myth" the DJJ devoted resources to, "breaking the cycle of poverty". They offer counseling through job related services, parenting classes and counseling of life skills. Poverty and crime are best addressed as a social issue and knowing the statistics and programs that work best for the youth will help prevent future involvement in the justice system and lower crime rates.

Youth detentions centers called, "secure detentions" located in a local facility or an "in-home detention program". "Male admissions accounted for 78 percent of all (Juvenile) detentions…. (FDJJ, 2006 pg. 58) Of the secure detentions in just Miami-Dade County, the non-Hispanic white male offender admissions were 261, the black offenders were 2,161, and the Hispanic white offenders were 1,442. The most reported crime among children in Florida is property offenses, being burglary, with 8,840 arrests. (FDJJ, 2006, p. 7). The second most reported crime by youth in the state of Florida is battery, with 15,786 arrests (FDJJ, 2006, p. 5). The third most reported are drug offenses with a total of 9,881 arrests (FDJJ, 2006, p. 9). It is not clear as to how poverty contributes to the outcome.

Although this is not a conclusive indication of poverty and crime in youth populations, it does suggest that poverty plays a role in crime, at least in Florida's largest metro area. Each year, the dept. releases a comprehensive evaluation of their services. Many statistics on the state level reports in terms of ethnicity and gender. Burglary, Assault & Battery and Drug offenses are a typical consequence of children living in impoverished communities.

This information presented challenges the hypothesis that children raised impoverished are more likely to be referred into the juvenile justice system versus children raised in middle class. It's believed the information gathered from the Department of Juvenile Justice itself dis-proved the hypothesis based on a lack of data to prove class disparities affected the outcome for Juveniles. Pertinent information would improve the results that class does have a negative result for impoverished children entering the DJJ. Mental health information is not so readily available to prove or dis-prove the validity of mental health for juveniles due to HIPAA laws. To solidify the hypothesis, it is suggested more than two sources of information should be provided based on household income.

References

1. Jens Ludwig, Greg J. Duncan, & Paul Hirschfield. (2001). Urban Poverty and Juvenile Crime: Evidence from a Randomized Housing-Mobility Experiment. The Quarterly Journal of Economics, (2), 655. Retrieved from http://search.ebscohost.com.proxy.ccis.edu/login.aspx?direct=true&db=edsjsr& AN=edsjsr.2696475&scope=site

2. Sitnick, S. L., Shaw, D. S., Weaver, C. M., Shelleby, E. C., Choe, D. E., Reuben, J. D., ... Taraban, L. (2017). Early Childhood Predictors of Severe

Youth Violence in Low-Income Male Adolescents. Child Development, 88(1), 27–40. https://doi-org.proxy.ccis.edu/10.1111/cdev.12680

3. Rekker, R., Pardini, D., Keijsers, L., Branje, S., Loeber, R., & Meeus, W. (2015). Moving in and out of Poverty: The Within- Individual Association between Socio-economic Status and Juvenile Delinquency. PLoS ONE, 10(11), 1. Retrieved from http://search.ebscohost.com.proxy.ccis.edu/login.aspx?direct=true&db=edb&AN=111057732&scope=site

4. Crosson-Tower, Cynthia. Exploring child welfare: a practice perspective. 7th ed., Pearson, 2018. New York, NY 10013

5. Florida Department of Juvenile Justice (2017). Comprehensive Accountability Report. Retrieved from http://www.djj.state.fl.us/research/reports/reports-and-data/static-research-reports/comprehensive-accountability-report

6. Florida Department of Juvenile Justice (2006). Outcome Evaluation Report [Data file]. Retrieved from http://www.djj.state.fl.us/research/reports/reports-and-data/static-research-reports/service-continuum-analysis

Chapter 4:

OUR MODERN HUMAN SERVICES

To state the importance of Human Services, one must define it. In An Introduction to Human Services by Woodside and McClam, Human Services presents as, "a professional approach to helping individuals, families, and communities address their unique needs". Abraham Maslow developed a hierarchy of needs in the 1940s that describe the basics of human needs through a theory of motivation. The greatest of the Maslow needs are physiological, safety, belongingness, esteem, then self-actualization as the least.

Poverty is a major component as it relates to Human Services. In fact, the US government defines poverty as an "insufficiency in food, housing, clothing, medical care, and other items required to maintain a decent standard of living." (DiNitto & Johnson) Of which, many people today live in or just above the poverty line. "Blacks are almost three times more likely to experience poverty than whites. Black children are the highest number of children living in poverty here in America." "35.7 percent of all black children live in poverty and the highest poverty rates occur in families headed by women where no husband is present." (DiNitto & Johnson) As education increases, poverty diminishes. "In 2009, the poverty rate for those with less than a high school diploma was 24.7 percent. Poverty among those with a bachelor's degree or more was 4.5 percent." (DiNitto & Johnson) The more people face poverty, the more Human Services that will be needed and depended on. Henceforth, the government has instituted funding and various programs to assist the needs of its citizens.

I chose Human Services as a profession to help people improve the quality of their life. As I have experienced life on the terms of lacking education, joblessness, and homelessness. I have witnessed and have too been affected by poverty. As stated earlier, black women and children have been inter-sectioned most historically as it pertains to poverty and human services. As many of my social counterparts and peers from childhood have succeeded; I and too many other black women have been left behind in the economic race. The latter has stunted the opportunity to attain a higher quality of life, freedom, and the pursuit of happiness here in America. As a Human Service Professional, I will strive to "acquire the knowledge and skills that can be transferred across settings and populations. Establish good working relationships with other professionals. Abide by the ethical standards that guide professional behavior. Pursue continuing education opportunities to learn and develop as a professional." (Woodside & McCam) From the time I was a teenager, I had always been passionate about helping other teens and have been able to relate to my peers.

I chose to enter the field on the premise of helping women and children because I, myself, have and still, I am overcoming many disparities of being inter-sectioned as a black woman. Having overcome the intergenerational trauma of being the scapegoat of a nation, I seek to show others how they too can discover their identity and to live a more purposed-driven life. The drive to help our youth work through the trauma of living in poverty and being unloved takes on another form of compassion. Teaching them how to effectively problem-solve in the environment they are, in numerous instances, neglected or abused in gives them the confidence to survive. We strongly believe there is a divine assignment for each person to carry out here in the earth. There is hope for an unknown future that is incorruptible. As African American people, although we have encountered a collective trauma yet, there is a collective healing of intergenerational trauma due to the legacy of slavery that shall rise from within the depths of who we are. This is the ascension we all have looked towards.

As a human service professional, I tackle many of the issues surrounding poverty in families, children, and economic development. I've done this through the development of a civic and social awareness nonprofit organization geared towards helping the issues of women and children. Because of the wide array of problems children (specifically, children of color) face while living in poverty; the organizational structure is project-based. Project-based allows for a designated number of people to tackle a myriad of issues simultaneously. Project-based also allows people to work without burnout. Project based allows a person to choose which projects he/she would best serve. By selecting one or more projects to bring forth cohesion to the black community, it is necessary for all to experience the joys of healing. Thus, permitting social acceptance and spreading awareness.

Our model focuses on a strengths-based approach. This is an approach to interventions that focuses on the positive attributes of the client and the client's environment. (Woodside & McClam) Pearls of Grace, Inc.

encourages a family approach to problem-solving. I envision families experiencing healing within the family unit, starting with the children. A 21-day drop center for runaway youth, in which it operates from a child-centered approach.

There is a major push for equality and equity in education. Due to the many disparities and unfair systems that negatively impact Black American children in the education system, Pearls of Grace, Inc. fights for education to become a civil liberty through the US Supreme Court system. Wealthy communities generally provide a better education for their children with lower taxes, rather than that of poorer communities paying a higher tax due to the property tax that varies one community to the next. By partnering with local citizens and school districts, we provide wrap-around services for families.

References
1.   An Introduction to Human Services, Eighth Edition by Marianne Woodside and Tricia McClam. Copyright © 2015, 2012 Cengage Learning
2.   Essentials of Social Welfare: Politics and Public Policy by Diana M. DiNitto and David H. Johnson. Copyright © 2012 Pearson Education, Inc.
3.   Politics in States and Communities (Thirteenth Edition) by Thomas R. Dye and Susan A MacManus. Copyright © 2009 Pearson/Prentice Hall
4.   Foundations of Democratic Education by Mary John O'Hair, H. James McLaughlin, Ulrich C. Reitzug. Copyright © 2000 by Harcourt, Inc.
5.   Maslow's hierarchy of needs. By: Aanstoos, Christopher M., Salem Press Encyclopedia of Health, 2013 Database: Research Starters

A.C.E.

In 2016, I lived in Orlando, Florida. I lived downtown, just one mile away from what's now known as OCPS Academy Center of Excellence acronym A.C.E.. It was a brand-new K-8 community school, and like many others, I eagerly watched Orange County Public Schools (OCPS) prepare for its grand opening for the 2017-2018 school year. The rumor was, school board member Dr. Kathleen Gordon played a major role in the school located on the outskirts of the highest poverty-stricken neighborhood in Orlando; Parramore. The economic challenges surrounding this historically black neighborhood categorized the school as Title 1. This allowed the project to receive additional state funding, and it was awarded over $60 million dollars. ACE was on its way to become known as one of the first community schools in Orange County.

The community welcomed A.C.E. as an addition to "Creative Village". A designated portion of land where the arts and education would collide among locals. Education institutions such as Valencia College, and the University of Central Florida partnered their way into the corridor and pledged to build a bridge of higher education for the citizens of Parramore. Local businesses, community interest groups, and citizens stood together with public declarations of how they too will link arms with one another for the uplifting of the Parramore district. To see this taking place was, by far, one of the highest acts of love I'd seen from a community!

It had been over 50 years since a neighborhood school had been within the district. Therefore, the children who attended A.C.E. were previously bussed to the 13 surrounding schools. So, when the school board announced that the school's architectural design included a pre-school, and medical offices for the neighborhood children; citizens were ecstatic as there was yet another reason to champion the school! Yet, as the project unfolded, there were several delays in the building process. For starters, the land selected was on top of a sinkhole. Thus, the infilling of it took a lot longer than the project anticipated. Next, builders dealt with situations that encompassed stolen materials from the work site. This delayed the project even further until many wondered if the school would be ready for the upcoming school year.

For months, I pondered to the Lord as to how I could make a difference in this movement. Then, one day, I received divine instruction to become a Substitute teacher. After completing the hiring process, I watched and waited. Miraculously, on the third day of school, an art teacher assignment opened at ACE! I jumped for it. The energy was high as the children were naturally getting acclimated to the new school. As I walked into the art class, I realized that there weren't any art supplies. So, we watch arts-based movies. I was asked to come back, and by the end of the week; the registrar asked if I would like to come back the following week, again, as the art teacher. I accepted, but by this time, I'd begun to hear rumors that the art teacher wasn't coming back.

That weekend, I spent time wrapping my head around what it would take for me to fill my new role successfully. I had two classes each period of the day. On Wednesdays, I had one hour of planning. After some research that weekend, I wrote my first week of elementary art curriculum from the Florida standards for my new K-5 throughout fifth grade students and centered it around identity. Yet, it was in our second week of school where teachers and administrators became aware that we might be in for a rude awakening! Walking on campus that week, was like walking into a beehive. Children were everywhere!

Teachers were screaming, students were fighting, and others were running aimlessly through the hallways. It was chaotic! As I walked by confrontational situations like I was walking through a minefield; I entered my classroom with a hint of anxiety. Deep down, I had a bad feeling about what was to come. From that point on, things got worse. For a few weeks, I was paired with a beautifully strict para-educator who helped tame poor behaviors from the children while I taught. Thankfully, she knew some students, and their parents, from her previous school. But, after she was pulled into a different class, it wasn't so easy for me to roundup the 40 something students each class period.

Before she left my class to be a support elsewhere, her, and I was selected to help file in administration one Wednesday on early release day. We arrived at an office where the files were in boxes and were left staggered across the office. As we began filing, I noticed these boxes had no order to them and that they were the children's files from the neighboring 13 schools who dropped them off the Friday before school started. My heart broke. As the two ladies spoke, I also learned that many of the parents had not been notified of the school's opening nor of their child's school transfer by the district. This also meant, that the administration had to figure out which children belonged there because many parents filed inaccurate address changes just to get their children into the new school. Then, everything clicked or me, as I now understood why large groups of angry parents filled the front office each morning.

Then, I wrote my first journal entry in almost two weeks. On August 29, 2017, I wrote, "I began my assignment about two weeks ago, but it feels like a month. I'm exhausted. No one prepared for what's going on here. Imagine filling an elementary academic environment with the most impoverished students. Not only are we dealing with the trauma associated with poverty but working with some of the severest forms of emotional neglect, and abuse in children is what's most difficult. I had never seen anything like what we are experiencing each day. One of my newest colleague friends (who'd taught for 20 years) said, she'd never even heard of anything like what we were experiencing. What makes matters even worse is that there's little to no leadership or support on how to properly handle these situations. Out of all the professionals who partnered with this community, why was no one ready to help us properly deal with the issues that are plaguing this community?"

In Parramore, it's common for single parent family units to have as many as seven, eight, or nine children. However, this breads conflict among other large family units within the community. Therefore, the fight for dominance transported itself from the community into the new learning environment. Many children who had IEPs weren't medicated. For the ones that were, many displayed a zombie effect. For the other children, the norm was to talk over teachers, throw school supplies around the classroom, and refuse to sit down; without disciplinary action taking place. One of the middle school deans told me one day, "Yesterday, there were 5 fights in middle school alone". He said, "if there are five fights or fewer in middle school a day; then we are doing well". Unfortunately, this environment became the norm all over the school. So much so, that A.C.E. began to be referred to as (Act Crazy Every day) among educators.

As time went on, I learned, many of the teachers who were hired, were not only first year teachers but were Caucasian. Then, I understood the correlation of statistical evidence in "stocking" of majority black schools with first year educators. Honestly, no matter how large their bonuses were and how much education they had, they simply weren't prepared for, nor did they know how to handle the behaviors of our children. Daily, they would walk through the hallways, often in a flighty daze. I would shake my head as I would notice their red tear-stained faces or outright witness the tears dropping. This unfortunately went on for months, but by the third week of school, educators begun to submit their resignation left and right. The trend continued well into the third month of school. According to some, the art teacher was smart to be the first one to get out. But, to me, I wondered, how could she not use the tools she had to help these children overcome their trauma? Even more-so, why did God allow a healing minister to come into their midst portrayed as an art teacher?

As the acting Art teacher, I instructed over 600 K—5th grader students a week. Unfortunately, the school did not prepare in ordering art supplies. So, I was given the crayons and markers that were donated to the school before school started. Subsequently, I barely got art supplies each week, and on a substitute teacher budget I purchased the remainder. The principal told me that he would reimburse me, but that never happened. Eventually, it got down to where admin asked me to cut construction paper in half just to supply for the need. Once that was gone, then I was rationed plain white paper in portions. Unfortunately, with over 600 students sharing the same Crayons and markers; within a few weeks they too had disintegrated.

Yet, little by little, the children began to grow accustomed to me. One day, one of my darling 6-year-olds walked up to me during class with a sad face and her head down. She mumbled in her sweet voice, "my picture ugly". It broke my heart. So, I asked, "who told you this?" She replied, "the girls at my table were laughing at my picture." I asked her to show me. She slowly pointed to her table. Then, I took her paper, put on my glasses, and examined her work of art for a moment. Next, I placed an enormous grin on my face, and I whispered, "It's a masterpiece!" She mumbled, "a masterpiece?" And, with a loud animated tone, I pointed my index finger upwards and said, "That's it! Of course, it's a masterpiece!" It was a moment I hoped she would never forget. After instructing her to repeat the phrase, "it's a masterpiece!" three times, each time louder than before; she convinced herself it was a masterpiece! She ran back to her table. Several minutes later, I saw her at the table raising her work of art saying, "Look, it's a masterpiece!"

On September 6, 2017, one of our second graders came up to me and in front of his teacher said, "I'm a stab you." After almost choking, I stood in disbelief as to what he told me and asked him to repeat what he said. He replied, "You heard me. I'm a stab you." I asked the teacher if she heard what he said, and she shrugged it off as like it was nothing. She proceeded on by telling me how she gets told much worse and how she was about to quit because she couldn't handle it anymore. We stood in silence for a moment, and she walked away.

Not too long after that, another educator told me that she had tried repeatedly to contact a guardian of one of her misbehaved children who was facing a suspension. When she finally contacted the guardian, the guardian told the teacher how she doesn't know why she keeps calling her because she can't do anything with the child at home either. The educator then told the teacher to figure it out and hung up.

When the superintendent and her assistant visited the campus, they were cursed out by students. Each time visit afterwards, educators were instructed to keep the children inside the classrooms throughout the duration of her visit. We resumed as normal afterwards her departure.

Although there were moments of extreme difficulty, we sought to make a difference. One day, one of my third graders told me that he wanted to be a fool, grow up to become a thug, and go to jail. Now, I knew he did not want this for himself, but I knew that this was the trend that he had become accustomed to seeing throughout his short life. After standing there looking eye to eye with him in silence, I told him how I don't want him to enter the classroom that day. I proceeded to act as if I was calling a police friend to come by the school to pick him up and take him in. I ask the student to skip every bad thing he was thinking about doing to save him and his family the heartache; just so he can go to jail that day. Surprisingly, at my initial gesture, he didn't flinch. So, I walked through the class to retrieve my cell phone and showed him a picture of myself with my police friend and said that was who I was calling to come get him. I could see the skepticism wipe away from his face. Then, I pretended to dial and speak to him as if he was on the phone with him. Next, the young man went into the classroom to sit down. I told him no, please sit by the door so that when the officer comes, he would not disrupt my class. The child surprisingly did what I asked. Throughout class, I didn't hear a word from him. As class wrapped up, he asked me if he could have a prize for being good. Unfortunately, I had given out all that I had, but I told him thank you for being on the best behavior that I had yet seen from him. He turned away with his head down, and I called him back. Then, I learned over and looked him in the eye and said, "You will not act like a fool, you will not grow up to be a thug, and you will not spend your life in jail. You will instead be smart and go to college, you will get married and have children, and you will become a judge and help other young men not go to jail." At that moment, a hush came over the class, and we looked at one another in the eyes until the teacher came in a called her class. Before leaving that day, he hugged me, and I never had a problem out of him again.

Yet, my worst experience with the children was when one of my second graders became enraged through an altercation with another student during class time. The dominant (injured by his ego from losing the fight) began pushing and throwing chairs around the classroom. From there, anything or anyone in his way was the recipient of his rage and was launched across the classroom. His rage ultimately led him to storm out of the classroom onto the playground. He eventually calmed down out there, but then he must have become enraged all over again by the thought of it. When he did, he wanted to come back for revenge. That's when I intervened by instructing the children to not open the doors, which allowed him back in. By this time, I had tried calling the front office for security repeatedly. By this point, I knew I had to handle it on my own.

As the situation progressed, the enraged child became violent because we wouldn't allow him back into the classroom, he began to beat on the windows and kick the emergency door. He kicked the door so hard and so many times that the $1000 door broke, and oil began leaking from it. That's when the children became afraid. Many of them huddled around me like chick's hover under a hen. Some latched on to me to where I couldn't move. Others hid under my desk, and the remainder hid into the supply closet. The boys stood guard at both doors to ensure he didn't get back in and even when the student was almost successful in entering, the boys gathered and pushed him out. I felt like I was in Area 51 and had never in my wildest dreams imagine one day being afraid of a second grader.

Immediately, after class I went to the office to speak to the principal and of course, he wasn't there. I told them I needed to speak to the elementary dean. She said there was none available because the acting dean had been nowhere to be found for weeks. I stood there in disbelief and told her that I needed to speak with someone. So, she took me to the mental health specialist, and I told her what had just transpired. She knew the student, and after relaying what had happened her response was the following: a child in his condition could not be suspended or even get into more trouble because he had already met the suspension maximum of 10 days per year, being that he had an IEP. She also stated, there was no alternative schooling, and that all we can do as educators is redirect him. Furthermore, she said even if he bought a knife to school, he would not be suspended or expelled.

When she said this, I began to weep because I knew it would be just a matter of time before another child would be inducted into the school to prison pipeline if something didn't change in his situation. Deep down I knew this was an issue that was bigger than the broken education system and even more-so something we had to face collectively as a people in our homes, in our schools, and in our communities.

Towards the end of the first quarter, I'd begun realizing how some of my first graders couldn't spell their last names. Some of my second graders couldn't spell sight words, and too many of my third graders couldn't spell simple words. Thereafter, I prayed for an opportunity to speak with the principal and on my last day of my assignment as the acting art teacher he walked down my hallway as I was packing up. I knew this was God. So, I asked for a few moments of his time to speak with him. He agreed. I began to share a couple of my concerns. I shared with him the nonprofit idea I felt God impressed upon my heart to start, and its central focus being education. Furthermore, I mentioned to him the tutoring aspect of the organization. His response to me was, "why don't you focus on going back to school to get your degree." I sat in silence as I didn't know whether to feel hurt or angered that out of everything I said, that was the best a principal with a Ph.D. Could respond with.

The following day, I was on my way to the Caribbean for a much-needed family vacation. Yet, with a heavy heart, I pondered with the Lord through the duration of the trip. When I returned to ACE, he was no longer the principal. Thankfully, as the year progressed under new leadership, some behaviors improved, but out of all these incidents it grew harder and harder to maintain the level of respect I once had for the education system. What made matters worse, was that, at the end of the school year there was a rumor that the administration missed the retention deadline therefore all the children who attended A.C.E. that year, were promoted to the next grade.

Chapter 5:

A MENTAL HEALTH OBSERVATION: MS. LATTIMORE

Ms. Lattimore is a 31-year-old African American female. She presents as well-groomed, self-controlled, and in good health. She has medical difficulty pertaining to early stages of lack of hearing in both ears. There appears to be fatigue, sadness, and anger that resides with her. She sleeps an average of 3-4 hours of sleep each night.

Ms. Lattimore owns her cleaning business and is a full-time student in her third year of college. While referencing her children, her content of thought included inconsistencies and several mild hallucinations. Her flow of thought exhibits a loss of short-term memory functions, and she admitted to hearing voices during various times. She recognizes her reasoning, insight, and judgement is cloudy, meaning inconsistent. She says she is not reliant on substance abuse and denies having suicidal ideations.

Ms. Lattimore is an only child, and due to her mother passing away as a young teenager, she was forced to relocate with her grandmother, the family matriarch. Through the series of unfortunate life downturns, Ms. Lattimore has had to revert to living with her grandmother.

Ms. Lattimore's family system is conflicting due to a strict religious home environment and her feelings of being, "unloved". She has four children, of which none are currently in her possession. She feels uncertain if she will get them back and feels alone when dealing with legal issues pertaining to them. Emotional support from family is nonexistent. However, her small sphere of peer relationships is emotionally supportive.

THE METHOD

Ms. Lattimore's diagnosis was most likely triggered when her children was removed from her custody. The strain of the situation sent her relationship into a downward spiral, leading to failure shortly afterwards. Going back to live with her grandmother was intimidating. Her options were to either live with her grandmother or be homeless. Having four children out of wedlock had already opened the door to an unhealthy psychological dynamic in her familial relationships. Growing up being the only child in an overly religious home environment, her behaviors were more often fixated on. There was constant criticism and disapproval of her behaviors, which caused her to experience downward emotional spirals. Her coping strategy is to (at times) adhere to the voices she hears in order to "survive".

Although, many African American traditions have been derived from religion and spirituality; judgement and condemnation are often imputed on to Ms. Lattimore due to her grandmother's strict adherence to her religious belief. She constantly feels as though she is not good enough to apprehend the "righteous" lifestyle her grandmother expects her to apprehend. Therefore, it leaves her living in a state of torment. Her grandmother's emotional, "coldness" leaves her feeling unloved and unsure of herself when it comes to motherhood. The reality of her not having her children in her custody validates the harsh treatment she has silently learned to accept from her grandmother. Ms. Lattimore's grandmother's belief and her lifestyle share such conflicting values that her grandmother's agenda and non-emotional support highly contributes to her digression.

How can Ms. Lattimore take on a whole new dimension of perceived thought about her life? Mentorship. A mentor can be more meaningful and clinically useful. A mentor can help her gain needed insight, knowledge, and support of her non-existent sense of identity. A mentor can also help her interpret her feelings and help her identify the root of where they originate from.

In Ms. Lattimore's situation, a woman who has experienced life on similar terms can help Ms. Lattimore confront disputed religious beliefs by helping her to discover her own foundational belief system instead of her grandmother's. This would allow her to process her emotions more so from a humanistic standpoint rather than as it pertains to religion. This increases her self-perception of value and alleviates traces of intergenerational condemnation.

A mentor's facilitated actions include implementing natural ways she can reclaim her power and improve her situation, beginning with her health. Upon evaluation, a mentor would discover Ms. Lattimore does not apprehend much sleep. Knowing how a prolonged lack of sleep could negatively impact the quality and trajectory of one's life. A mentor would help Ms. Lattimore discover and implement healthy options as to how she could overcome her sleep irregularities. Aroma therapy, relaxation techniques such as meditating and stretching would be natural ways to help ease her symptoms of anxiety. A mentor would help facilitate a series of art-based sessions where the mentee could consistently portray her feelings through imagery and transference. To deal with the root issues, mentor/mentee develops short-term and long-term goals in a non-intrusive approach to help implement a consistent plan of action.

THE RESULTS

After short-term and long-term goals was developed, Ms. Lattimore agreed to become more educated on diet and the importance of improving her environment. She ate greener and began taking melatonin for consistent sleeping patterns. She and her mentor built a systematic daily management calendar centered around her disability. Furthermore, she also agreed to start to journaling for self-monitoring of positive/negative thought patterns and emotions; in which they reviewed certain aspects of the journaling process together. Ms. Lattimore strengthened her social skills by initiating friendships at school and joined her local chamber of commerce to increase her flow of business and foster new relationships outside her grandmother's circle of influence. Discussing, researching, and implementing coping skills increases the value of mentoring sessions along with adequate tracking.

Over a period of seven-months, Ms. Lattimore gained a better understanding of her identity and was empowered enough to begin speaking up for herself among her relatives. Over the next several months, the focus is to improve Ms. Lattimore's quality of life would be independence.

References
1. Title: Schizophrenia. By: Piotrowski, Nancy A., Ph.D., Tischauser, Leslie V., Ph.D., Magill's Medical Guide (Online Edition), 2013. Database: Research Starters
2. Title: Natural treatments for schizophrenia. By: EBSCO CAM Review Board, Salem Press Encyclopedia of Health, 2013. Database: Research Starters

Chapter 6:

AN ADDICTION OBSERVATION: EBONY

The Role of Culture in the Assessment and Treatment of Substance Abuse with an individual is an important factor to consider for both the clinician and the client.

High Schooler Ebony is a 15-year-old African American female in the inner city of Bronx, NY. Although her mother works a full-time job, she receives government assistance to help meet the family's needs. Ebony is the oldest of three siblings and has recently been locked up at the juvenile detention center for stealing. She admitted to the courts of her dependence on marijuana and alcoholic substances she gets from older friends. She also admitted that she was drunk and high at the time she was caught stealing. Ebony was assigned a case manager as a condition of the courts and must now meet with her case manager twice a week.

Samantha, a middle-aged woman with a MSW

retrieves the case and quickly becomes a central figure in Ebony's life. Samantha has been in this role for about five years and has a higher-than-normal success rate for teens in similar situations such as Ebony. Many of her colleagues account it from her approach and willingness to, "get to the nitty-gritty" with her clients (something they shy away from). However, Samantha enjoys seeing the rewards after the work has been put in. Immediately, Samantha organizes a pre-counseling session to get to know her client a little better. There she allows personal space for and encourages Ebony to dream, to goal set and the plan. The session sounds easier than it is, due to Ebony's feelings of a depleted childhood because of her responsibility to watch after her younger siblings.

Samantha carefully examined the needs of service according to Ebony's daily life and case expectations. For emotional support, Samantha organized for Ebony to attend group counseling for inner-city teens weekly. Their teens would be able to work in groups to express their cultural pain through artistic expressions. Samantha showed an appreciation for cultural arts and what they mean to Structurally Traumatized communities. For Ebony's education requires, Samantha guaranteed Ebony a seat at the next substance abuse education workshop each Saturday and for four Saturdays following.

Because of Ebony's mother's work schedule, Ebony can only participate in weekend activities to fulfill her obligations with the courts. However, speaking with Ebony's mom Shaina, she agreed to do her best in planning for a babysitter one night a week. Yet! Instead, Samantha spoke to the agency Director and advocated for an organization volunteer to stay one hour later to watch Ebony's siblings at the aftercare center during her counseling session. Her Programed Director agreed, while Samantha ordered a $5 pizza from Little Cesar's for the children to eat during the counseling session. Samantha's organization and commitment to providing a need for the wellbeing of her client-built trust with Ebony's family. It also taught Ebony more responsibility and served as a reward system of service as an incentive to put her needs above enforced familial duties.

Samantha was agreeing with why she was working in this community. To be successful with this case, Samantha had to release the negative stigma associated with working with most African American women who was dealing with addiction, bias, and anger. She believed that Ebony fell prey to the systemic charge and therefore could possibly become a product of her environment if there is not an effective intervention. Samantha demonstrated empathy for Ebony and her family by staying an extra hour each Wednesday, orchestrating a volunteer to watch the siblings and ensuring they had dinner while providing counseling services to Ebony.

Over the course of the first month of counseling, Samantha began to see signs of mental health instability. Ebony had not ever been diagnosed with anything, but Samantha had reason to believe Ebony was dealing with unidentified trauma. Samantha was well-educated on cultural bias and completed the assessment, knowing based on research how easy it would be to misdiagnose signs of cultural trauma for other mental health symptoms. After completing the assessment, Samantha's assumptions about Ebony's trauma were correct. Samantha went over the results during the following counseling session, and there she engaged Ebony in self-discovery exercises and presented options for treatment.

After much thought and researching community resources, they both agreed on after the Saturday substance abuse education workshops, Ebony would begin attending community rites of passage program for teenaged girls. The program would be derived from African culture and traditions to the African American experience. Samantha believed this type of program would build a bridge of hope into Ebony's circumstances. From there, she would learn more about the struggles she faces as a woman of color and would be able to relate to her mother and other women of color. Upon completion of the program, Ebony would have an opportunity to partner with the organization by becoming a student activist in her community. This would help develop her leadership skills and ultimately rebuild the community that had for generations systemically oppressed her and her family.

In conclusion, because of Samantha's realistic approach and ability to organize, she helped a family reconnect to themselves and enhanced the future outcome of a young lady who could have been lost in the system. Yet, due to her cultural sensitivity, Samantha was able to redirect Ebony's focus from coping with substance abuse to finding hope, purpose, and action to make a better future for herself. Ebony took responsibility of her actions, discovered hope in her daily living situation, and became a sound of resiliency for her community. By the end of treatment, Ebony stated that she no longer wanted to drink or get high. The group of friends she once had were no longer apart from her life and she had found new friends and has now begun working on her self-confidence. Ebony was on the track to success and is now considering college as a goal and possibility in her future.

The difference between Ebony and a Native American 15-year-old living on a reservation who suffered from substance abuse addiction would be geographical. Although both had most likely encountered trauma, Ebony had no previous knowledge of her identity. Therefore, she is more susceptible to sway in her decision-making skills based upon social influences; wherein the Native girl had a working knowledge and understanding of her identity. In communal settings, there are also celebrations and oral traditions as reminders of her identity. Ebony did not know who she was culturally, nor could she identify the generational struggles in which she lived daily. I believe there would be more room to discover in both situations.

Resources

1. Williams, I. L. . (2016). The intersection of structurally traumatized communities and substance use treatment: Dominant discourses and hidden themes. Journal of Ethnicity in Substance Abuse, 15(2), 95–126. https://doi-org.proxy.ccis.edu/10.1080/15332640.2014.1003671

2. Melnick, G., Duncan, A., Thompson, A., Wexler, H. K., Chaple, M., & Cleland, C. M. (2011). Racial Disparities in Substance Abuse Treatment and the Ecological Fallacy. Journal of Ethnicity in Substance Abuse, 10(3), 226–245. https://doi-org.proxy.ccis.edu/10.1080/15332640.2011.600201

3. Meshberg-Cohen, S., Presseau, C., Thacker, L. R., Hefner, K., & Svikis, D. (2016). Posttraumatic Stress Disorder, Health Problems, and Depression Among African American Women in Residential Substance Use Treatment. Journal of Women's Health (15409996), 25(7), 729–737. https://doi-org.proxy.ccis.edu/10.1089/jwh.2015.5328

4. Amaro, H., Larson, M. J., Gampel, J., Richardson, E., Savage, A., & Wagler, D. (2005). Racial/ethnic differences in social vulnerability among women with co-occurring mental health and substance abuse disorders: Implications for treatment services. Journal of Community Psychology, 33(4), 495–511. https://doi-org.proxy.ccis.edu/10.1002/jcop.20065

5. Poitier VL, & Niliwaaambieni M. (1997). A rite of passage approach designed to preserve the families of substance-abusing African American Women. Child Welfare, 76(1), 173–195. Retrieved from https://proxy.ccis.edu/login?url=http://search.ebscohost.com/login.aspx?direct=true&db=c8h&AN=106102190&scope=site

Chapter 7:

THE REVELATION

I didn't know what to expect before arriving in Geneva, Switzerland, but I was anxious. The grandeur of the city's name and it being known as the world's headquarters for peace had me in a 48-hr. cycle of suspense. I was a little unearthed as I felt that there was something there, I was supposed to find, discover, or connect with. What exactly? I didn't know. And, as our departure date drew closer, I experienced little to no sleep, and a prompting to begin fasting. I began asking God to reveal His will and for the ability to hear clear directions. I reached out to my sisters back home and requested prayer.

We arrived, checked in, and was off to explore Geneva. I instantly fell in love with the city as our small group defaulted to our plan B, touring the Red Cross Museum. In class, we learned how the Red Cross played a major role during and after World War 1. The founder, Henry Dunant, was from Switzerland. He and his partners took the charge of becoming an intermediary in connecting lost loved ones who died or went missing. I was curious to learn more. At the beginning of the second exhibition, I grasped for a greater understanding where an engraved stone on the wall contained the words, "Restoring the Family Links" in French, English, and German. As I walked through, there were chains hanging from the ceiling. I must admit that I was slightly confused at the meaning of what this display was depicting. I began to question, slavery? But then, I realized this had everything to do with war, not slavery. After I walked through the hanging chains, there were massive cases of glass covered shelving with rows of what they called catalogs. There were thousands of small 3×5 cards carefully preserved inside little wooden boxes. Several steps, thereafter, were open displays preceding a scaled wall that contained dozens of pictures with small children of color. Yet, it was in those moments I received fresh revelation that led me to question God with a series of questions. My first question was, Father, why is there not a system in place commemorating and reconnecting those who are descendants of the diaspora to Africa?" Then, I solemnly asked, "Why are there not catalogs leading us back to our tribesmen back home?" Finally, I asked, "Father, why, after 400 years are our family links not restored?"

Within a few moments, my body began to burn with righteous anger. Next, I was filled with sadness and grief at all that has been lost in the diaspora. It was there, I was left to deal with the painful reality that America is my birth country but not my home. My pace slowed down as I came to a halt on a bench near the end of the self-guided tour. As I sat, I was faced with emotion and felt alone. To shake it off, I encouraged myself to walk through the final exhibition. It was called, Prison. The exhibition was like a prison capsule that allowed visitors to walk through to learn about social in-justice and punishment worldwide. There were sound-overs and film recordings; metal bars and steel entry doorways; statistics and interactive modules. As I moved through the exhibit, there was a graph that demonstrated how the United States housed the most prisoners worldwide, majority African Americans. I became overwhelmed with emotion after seeing how the artist depicted the numbers (in 2019) at this magnitude. I froze and within seconds I began to shake from the inside out. Dizziness came upon me, and I felt a slight sickening feeling in my stomach. I clenched my torso area and told God how sick I now felt. Then, the words, "school to prison pipeline" arose from within my spirit. As I proceeded onwards towards the exit, I paused to sit down at the finale, and there I briefly watched one of the short black and white films that vividly depicted prisoners and how they coped with incarceration while incarcerated. Now nauseated and grasping for breath, I ran out of the exhibit, crying out to the Lord. After a series of open visions, I heard the Holy Spirit say, "Do you see how bad you feel about this? I replied under my breath, "yes." He then said, "How do you think I feel?" From that point, I was undone! After purging, He said, "Go back and make the change". When I heard that, He sealed up my emotions like a package, and instantly I was back to myself.

At dinner, my professor requested a recap from us students and as my Caucasian peers shared their outlook; I withheld mine. Truly, I wanted to avoid expressing my version of the experience because I knew I was located at the far end of their spectrum. Regardless of how I felt, I proceeded to share my outlook in a solemn mannerism. Yet, I could not stop the pain from spewing out from the corridors of my heart through the opening of my mouth. I spoke not of my interpretation, but of my personal experiences in dealing with the criminal justice system. An awkward silence brushed over the table as I finished speaking as I came to the realization that the table was taking an introspective look at the emotional vomit, I just spewed out over our dinner table. Strangely, I felt better after saying it and was gratified by their introspection. The trauma in dealing with the U.S. mass incarceration phenomenon has left the African American family unit to endure another feat of collective trauma. In the 21st century, it is far worse that the legacy of slavery. It is slavery.

As an African American, I'd have to admit that it has been excruciating these past few years to see the levels of turmoil on the rise in our society. Multitudes of African Americans sit privately in pain, while others directly impacted voice their cry for help. Yet, it seems the world continues to ignore and profit from mass incarceration.

There is a scripture in the book of Matthew of the Bible. At the end of the parable of the sheep and goat, it says, "The King will reply, 'Truly I tell you, whatever you did for one of the least of these brothers and sisters of mine, you did for me…. Truly, I tell you, whatever you did not do for one of the least of these, you did not do for me. Then they will go away to eternal punishment, but the righteous to eternal life.'" — Matthew 25:31-46 NIV

Visiting the Red Cross Museum was an experience I will never forget. Although my time in Geneva was hardly enough, in more ways than one did I feel great sadness upon leaving. Geneva is my place of solace. A place that I will hold within my heart.

MORAL OBLIGATION

German philosopher and enlightenment thinker Immanuel Kant says that the only thing that is "wholly good", in and of itself and that matters, is the intent of the will. In that, the purity of one's intentions brings the highest good of all. Kant's supreme moral principle is best known as the golden rule which is to in best words, "love your neighbor as yourself" – Mark 12:31. The practical version of the principle is to treat others only in the way you yourself would want to be treated in every situation. This belief system would argue, racist acts would and should be irrelevant based on the moral worth that every individual should be operating on the intent of their will for the highest good of all, through the power of love.

Aristotle's argument would most likely be that racism is more often infiltrated into a child's character through parental teaching and observation. And, Mill's Utilitarianism would probably argue it is the responsibility of the population majority to govern the moral right to determine social acceptance of who inflicts acts of racism towards the minority racial class. Yet, what is the greater good?

The moral issue plaguing the US & the world today is racism. Yes, ethics has been used as a major player to bring forth progress in race relations in the U.S. However, the power of a pure intention can cut through the most potent environments to dismember all elements. I have a contribution in the form of a solution.

Chapter 8:

THE SOLUTION: PEARLS OF GRACE, INC.

Pregnancy & Birthing

All medical staff should undergo cultural education and intervention training to produce better African American female pregnancy outcomes. Then, developing national social awareness geared towards helping pregnant African American mothers reduce stress throughout the duration of their pregnancy.

Child Trauma Groups

After school small groups for children to help one another process and cope with trauma that pertain to everyday survival scenarios in their world. Small group volunteerism would consist of providing homework help and mentoring for students. Members of Pearls of Grace, Inc. undergo training to ensure proper facilitation and avenues of healing among our children.

Therapeutic Art Sessions

Sessions to artistically engage children in group setting help students to practice transference of emotion into tangible meaning. Community cultural art projects, music, storytelling, and role playing are just a few ways students and parents can adhere to exploring change. Mindfulness, coping, self-esteem building, and resiliency are all factors incorporated in each session.

Equestrienne Therapy

Research studies are now showing how effective equestrienne therapy also known as hippotherapy is helping people with physical disabilities, psychological disorders (such as Anxiety, PTSD, Autism, etc.) and emotional disorders. Pearls of Grace, Inc. would like to incorporate equestrienne therapy to assist in the process of intergenerational healing.

Addiction Recovery

Utilizing methods of Prevention and Harm Reduction programing in addiction recovery environments are appropriate for individuals to learn how to apply self-care techniques to prevent alcohol or illicit drug abuse. Cultural awareness should be applied.

Intergenerational Healing

Members come together to look introspectively at intergenerational healing for themselves and their families. Due to the legacy of slavery, this platform helps black women finally rise out of national intergenerational scapegoat-ism to reclaim her voice and power through civic engagement and social awareness advocacy.

Community Development

Developing communities that will provide affordable housing alternatives, entrepreneurial training, wholistic lifestyles, and rediscovering our identity by faith.

ABOUT THE AUTHOR

A black woman.

Made in the USA
Columbia, SC
26 September 2024